Survey of Law School Faculty 2025, Views of Online Legal Education

ISBN 979-8-88517-291-2

Table of contents

THE QUESTIONNAIRE

1. Please give us the following contact information:

   A. Name:
   B. Organization:
   C. Title
   D. Email address:

2. You are:

   A. Professor
   B. Assistant/Associate Professor
   C. Lecturer or Research Fellow
   D. Adjunct/Clinical Faculty
   E. Emeritus
   F. Other (please specify)

3. How old are you?

   A. Under 30
   B. 30-39
   C. 40-49
   D. 50-59
   E. 60 or Over

4. Are you male or female?

   A. Male
   B. Female
   C. Transgender

5. Your law school has approximately how many students?

6. Is your law school public or private?

   A. Public
   B. Private

7. In the past semester how many courses did you teach?

   A. None
   B. One
   C. Two
   D. More than Two

8. Which phrase best approximates the view of your law school taken by organizations that rank law schools?

A. Top 20 law school
B. Somewhere in the 21-75 rank
C. 76 to 250
D. Other

9. Which phrase best characterizes your political beliefs?

A. Right of Conservative
B. Conservative
C. Centrist
D. Liberal
E. Left of Liberal
F. Curriculum Development

10. Have you ever taught any of the following? (check all that apply)

A. Fully online law course during the Pandemic
B. Fully online law course prior to or after the Pandemic
C. Hybrid law course during the Pandemic
D. Hybrid law course during the Pandemic

11. Have you taught an online or hybrid legal course within the past year?

A. Yes
B. No

12. In general what do you think of the general quality of online legal education relative to traditional courses at your institution?

A. Much better
B. Better
C. About the same
D. Worse
E. Much worse

13. How extensively is your law school using online legal education?

A. A great deal
B. A lot
C. A moderate amount
D. A little
E. None at all

14. Do you agree: My law school should significantly increase its use of online legal education.

A. Strongly agree
B. Agree
C. Neither agree nor disagree
D. Disagree
E. Strongly disagree

15. How and for what should online legal education be used at your institution?

Characteristics of the sample

Academic title

	#
Professor	61
Assistant/Associate Professor	21
Adjunct/Clinical Faculty	28
Emeritus	15
Other	9
Total	134

Age of respondent

	#
Under 40	6
40-49	19
50-59	33
60 or over	75
Unknown	1
Total	134

Gender of respondent

	#
Male	80
Female	50
Other	4
Total	134

Public or private law school

	#
Public	81
Private	53
Total	134

# of courses taught last semester

	#
None	27
One	40
Two	59
More than two	8
Total	134

Approximate Self Assessed Law School Ranking

	#
Top 20 law school	27
Somewhere in the 21-75 rank	55
76 to 250	46
Other	6
Total	134

Political views

	#
Conservative	14
Centrist	34
Liberal	65
Left of Liberal	20
Unknown	1
Total	134

Law school enrollment size

	#
Less than 400	32
400+ - 550	32
550+ - 800	34
More than 800	36
Total	134

INSTITUTIONAL AFFILIATIONS OF THE SURVEY PARTICIPANTS

Belmont University College of Law
Benjamin N. Cardozo School of Law
Bennett Law Firm
Boston University School of Law
Buffalo State University
Cardozo
Carey Law, U Maryland
Charleston School of Law
Chicago-Kent
Columbia Law School
Creighton University School of Law
Duke Law
Emory University
Fisher Broyles
Fordham Law School
Fordham University School of Law
Harvard Law School
Howard University
Indiana University
Kern High School District
LMU Loyola Law School
Louisiana State Univ. Law Center
LSU Law Center Juvenile Defense Clinic
LSU Law, Tulane law
Marquette University Law School
MC Law
McGill University
Mercer Univ. School of Law
Mississippi Supreme Court
Mitchell Hamline School of Law
MSU College of Law
New England Law | Boston
Northeastern University School of Law
Northern Illinois University College of Law
Northwestern Law School
OU Law
Pace Law School
Pepperdine Caruso Law
Roger Williams University School of Law
Rutgers Law School
Salesforce, Inc.
Santa Clara University School of Law
Schulich School of Law
SMU Law School
Southern University Law Center
St. Mary's University School of Law
Stetson University College of Law

Temple Law School
The Ohio State University Moritz College of Law
The University of Tennessee College of Law
Thomas Jefferson School of Law
Thurgood Marshall S of Law
UCI law
UCLA School of Law
UGA School of Law
UIC Law
UMass Law School
UMKC Law School
UNC-CH
Univ. of Washington School of Law
University of Arkansas
University of California Irvine Law School
University of California San Francisco law
University of Connecticut Law School
University of Florida
University of Georgia School of Law
University of Idaho
University of Illinois Chicago Law School
University of Iowa, College of Law
University of Maryland School of Law
University of Mississippi, School of Law
University of Nebraska - Lincoln College of Law
University of North Carolina School of Law
University of Oklahoma College of Law
University of Oregon School of Law
University of Richmond
University of South Dakota Law School
University of St. Thomas -- Minnesota
University of Tennessee
University of Texas
University of Toronto
University of Tulsa
University of Virginia
University of Wyoming
UT Law and Bush School
UVA Law
UW School of Law
Villanova University
Washington Univ in St Louis
Wayne State Law School
Wayne State University Law School
William S. Boyd School of Law, UNLV
Wise Law Library, CU Boulder
Yale Law School

SUMMARY OF MAIN FINDINGS

Experience Teaching Online or Hybrid Courses

Online Courses During the Pandemic:

- 64.93% of respondents taught a fully online law course during the pandemic, while 35.07% had not.
- Professors (80.33%) were the most likely to have taught online, while adjunct/clinical faculty (53.57%) and emeritus faculty (46.67%) were less likely.
- Faculty at larger law schools (more than 800 students) had the highest participation rate (77.78%) compared to smaller law schools (<400 students: 62.50%).
- Younger faculty (under 40: 33.33%) were significantly less likely to have taught online than those aged 50-59 (78.79%).
- Women (72.00%) were more likely than men (58.75%) to have taught online.
- Faculty at private law schools (73.58%) were more likely than those at public institutions (59.26%) to have taught an online course.

Online Courses Before or After the Pandemic:

- 26.12% had taught a fully online law course before or after the pandemic, while 73.88% had not.
- Senior faculty (professors: 37.70%) were more likely than assistant/associate professors (14.29%) to have taught online outside of the pandemic period.
- Larger law schools (800+ students: 47.22%) had higher pre/post-pandemic adoption than smaller schools (<400 students: 21.88%).
- Women (36.00%) were more likely than men (20.00%) to have taught online courses before or after the pandemic.

Hybrid Courses During the Pandemic:

- 33.58% of faculty taught a hybrid law course during the pandemic, while 66.42% had not.
- Professors (49.18%) were far more likely than adjunct/clinical faculty (21.43%) to have taught hybrid courses.
- Faculty at larger law schools (800+ students: 41.67%) were more likely to have taught hybrid courses.
- Private law school faculty (45.28%) had a higher rate of hybrid teaching than public law school faculty (25.93%).
- Only 11.94% had taught a hybrid law course before or after the pandemic, while 88.06% had not.
- Professors (18.03%) were more likely than adjunct/clinical faculty (3.57%) to have done so.

  - Faculty at the largest law schools (800+ students: 27.78%) were significantly more likely than those at mid-sized law schools (400-800 students: <4%) to have taught hybrid courses before or after the pandemic.

Recent Online or Hybrid Teaching Experience

- In the past year, 21.64% of faculty had taught an online or hybrid legal course, while 69.40% had not.
- Faculty at larger law schools (800+ students: 33.33%) were more active in recent online teaching than those at smaller schools.
- Women (22.00%) were slightly more likely than men (20.00%) to have taught online in the past year.
- Private law school faculty (26.42%) had higher participation in online/hybrid teaching than their public law school counterparts (18.52%).

Perceptions of the Quality of Online Legal Education

- 55.97% of faculty believed online legal education was of lower quality than traditional in-person courses, while only 9.7% rated it as better.
- Senior professors (39.34%) were more likely to rate online education as "worse" than adjuncts (32.14%).
- Faculty at public law schools (41.98%) were slightly more critical than those at private institutions (33.96%).
- Politically conservative faculty were the most critical, with 64.29% rating online legal education as "worse" or "much worse."

Extent of Law School Use of Online Education

- 70.15% of respondents reported that their law schools used online education "a little" or "moderately."
- Faculty at the largest law schools (800+ students) reported the highest levels of online education use (19.44% reported "a lot" or "a great deal").
- Adjunct faculty (28.57%) reported the highest use of online education at their institutions.

Level of Faculty Support for Expanding Online Legal Education

- 53.99% of faculty opposed significantly increasing online education, while 21.64% supported it.
- Younger faculty (40-49: 21.05% support) were more open to expansion than older faculty (60+: 13.33% support).

Qualitative Findings from Open-Ended Responses

Theme	Summary of Responses
Opposition to Online Legal Education	Many faculty argued that online legal education is a poor substitute for in-person instruction, citing diminished engagement, ineffective Zoom-based teaching, and a lack of meaningful interpersonal interactions. Some stated that students are "being shortchanged" and that "online education is inferior in every way."
Support for Limited Use	Some faculty suggested that online education has merit for certain applications, such as continuing legal education (CLE), certificate programs, and supplemental instruction. Others recommended its use for remote guest speakers or in situations where in-person instruction is not feasible due to weather emergencies.
Hybrid Models and Blended Learning	A number of responses suggested that hybrid learning could be a useful tool for increasing flexibility, particularly for part-time or working students. However, many emphasized that it should not replace traditional classroom experiences.
Improving Online Education	Some faculty recommended improving online legal education through better training, more interactive course designs, and the integration of AI-based tutoring. A few suggested that "high-quality asynchronous courses could be beneficial, but most current offerings are low-quality."
Expanding Access	A small number of respondents highlighted that online education could help expand legal education to underserved communities or students with disabilities. However, they cautioned that online programs must maintain high educational standards to be truly beneficial.
Administrative and Financial Considerations	Several faculty members expressed concerns that online education is driven by financial incentives rather than pedagogical quality. Some viewed it as "a profit-maker rather than a legitimate educational tool," and argued that law schools should resist the pressure to increase online offerings simply for revenue generation.
Use Cases for Online Legal Education	Responses from mid-ranked and lower-ranked law schools showed more openness to online courses for summer sessions, electives, and specialized courses that are difficult to staff in-person. Some also mentioned the potential for collaboration across institutions via online courses.

Findings

The survey reveals a strong division in attitudes toward online legal education. While many faculty members acknowledge its utility in specific contexts—such as hybrid learning, CLE programs, and remote guest lectures—there is widespread skepticism about its overall quality compared to in-person instruction. Resistance is particularly high among senior faculty, faculty at top-ranked law schools, and those with conservative political views. Conversely, younger faculty, adjunct faculty, and those at private law schools show slightly greater acceptance of online legal education, especially in blended formats or for specialized purposes. Any future expansion of online legal education will likely require significant improvements in course quality, training, and student engagement to gain broader faculty support.

Table 1 Have you ever taught any of the following? (check all that apply)

Table 1.1.1 Have you ever taught any of the following? Fully online law course during the Pandemic.

	No Answer	Yes	No
Entire sample	0.00%	64.93%	35.07%

Table 1.1.2 Have you ever taught any of the following? Fully online law course during the Pandemic. Broken out by law school enrollment

Law school enrollment	Yes	No
Less than 400	62.50%	37.50%
400+ - 550	53.13%	46.88%
550+ - 800	64.71%	35.29%
More than 800	77.78%	22.22%

Table 1.1.3 Have you ever taught any of the following? Fully online law course during the Pandemic. Broken out by academic title

Academic title	Yes	No
Professor	80.33%	19.67%
Assistant/Associate Professor	57.14%	42.86%
Adjunct/Clinical Faculty	53.57%	46.43%
Emeritus	46.67%	53.33%
Other	44.44%	55.56%

Table 1.1.4 Have you ever taught any of the following? Fully online law course during the Pandemic. Broken out by age of respondent

Age of respondent	Yes	No
Under 40	33.33%	66.67%
40-49	57.89%	42.11%
50-59	78.79%	21.21%
60 or over	62.67%	37.33%
Unknown	100.00%	0.00%

Table 1.1.5 Have you ever taught any of the following? Fully online law course during the Pandemic. Broken out by gender of respondent

Gender of respondent	Yes	No
Male	58.75%	41.25%
Female	72.00%	28.00%
Other	100.00%	0.00%

Table 1.1.6 Have you ever taught any of the following? Fully online law course during the Pandemic. Broken out by public or private law school

Public or private law school	Yes	No
Public	59.26%	40.74%
Private	73.58%	26.42%

Table 1.1.7 Have you ever taught any of the following? Fully online law course during the Pandemic. Broken out by # of courses taught last semester

# of courses taught last semester	Yes	No
None	44.44%	55.56%
One	70.00%	30.00%
Two	72.88%	27.12%
More than two	50.00%	50.00%

Table 1.1.8 Have you ever taught any of the following? Fully online law course during the Pandemic. Broken out by ranking

Ranking	Yes	No
Top 20 law school	55.56%	44.44%
Somewhere in the 21-75 rank	67.27%	32.73%
76 to 250	67.39%	32.61%
Other	66.67%	33.33%

Table 1.1.9 Have you ever taught any of the following? Fully online law course during the Pandemic. Broken out by political views

political views	Yes	No
Conservative	71.43%	28.57%
Centrist	61.76%	38.24%
Liberal	66.15%	33.85%
Left of Liberal	60.00%	40.00%
Unknown	100.00%	0.00%

Table 1.2.1 Have you ever taught any of the following? Fully online law course prior to or after the Pandemic.

	No Answer	Yes	No
Entire sample	0.00%	26.12%	73.88%

Table 1.2.2 Have you ever taught any of the following? Fully online law course prior to or after the Pandemic. Broken out by law school enrollment

Law school enrollment	Yes	No
Less than 400	21.88%	78.13%
400+ - 550	18.75%	81.25%
550+ - 800	14.71%	85.29%
More than 800	47.22%	52.78%

Table 1.2.3 Have you ever taught any of the following? Fully online law course prior to or after the Pandemic. Broken out by academic title

Academic title	Yes	No
Professor	37.70%	62.30%
Assistant/Associate Professor	14.29%	85.71%
Adjunct/Clinical Faculty	21.43%	78.57%
Emeritus	6.67%	93.33%
Other	22.22%	77.78%

Table 1.2.4 Have you ever taught any of the following? Fully online law course prior to or after the Pandemic. Broken out by age of respondent

Age of respondent	Yes	No
Under 40	16.67%	83.33%
40-49	36.84%	63.16%
50-59	27.27%	72.73%
60 or over	24.00%	76.00%
Unknown	0.00%	100.00%

Table 1.2.5 Have you ever taught any of the following? Fully online law course prior to or after the Pandemic. Broken out by gender of respondent

Gender of respondent	Yes	No
Male	20.00%	80.00%
Female	36.00%	64.00%
Other	25.00%	75.00%

Table 1.2.6 Have you ever taught any of the following? Fully online law course prior to or after the Pandemic. Broken out by public or private law school

Public or private law school	Yes	No
Public	22.22%	77.78%
Private	32.08%	67.92%

Table 1.2.7 Have you ever taught any of the following? Fully online law course prior to or after the Pandemic. Broken out by # of courses taught last semester

# of courses taught last semester	Yes	No
None	14.81%	85.19%
One	25.00%	75.00%
Two	33.90%	66.10%
More than two	12.50%	87.50%

Table 1.2.8 Have you ever taught any of the following? Fully online law course prior to or after the Pandemic. Broken out by ranking

Ranking	Yes	No
Top 20 law school	18.52%	81.48%
Somewhere in the 21-75 rank	29.09%	70.91%
76 to 250	26.09%	73.91%
Other	33.33%	66.67%

Table 1.2.9 Have you ever taught any of the following? Fully online law course prior to or after the Pandemic. Broken out by political views

Political views	Yes	No
Conservative	42.86%	57.14%
Centrist	26.47%	73.53%
Liberal	27.69%	72.31%
Left of Liberal	10.00%	90.00%
Unknown	0.00%	100.00%

Table 1.3.1 Have you ever taught any of the following? Hybrid law course during the Pandemic.

	No Answer	Yes	No
Entire sample	0.00%	33.58%	66.42%

Table 1.3.2 Have you ever taught any of the following? Hybrid law course during the Pandemic. Broken out by law school enrollment

Law school enrollment	Yes	No
Less than 400	31.25%	68.75%
400+ - 550	31.25%	68.75%
550+ - 800	29.41%	70.59%
More than 800	41.67%	58.33%

Table 1.3.3 Have you ever taught any of the following? Hybrid law course during the Pandemic. Broken out by academic title

Academic title	Yes	No
Professor	49.18%	50.82%
Assistant/Associate Professor	33.33%	66.67%
Adjunct/Clinical Faculty	21.43%	78.57%
Emeritus	13.33%	86.67%
Other	0.00%	100.00%

Table 1.3.4 Have you ever taught any of the following? Hybrid law course during the Pandemic. Broken out by age of respondent

Age of respondent	Yes	No
Under 40	33.33%	66.67%
40-49	21.05%	78.95%
50-59	45.45%	54.55%
60 or over	32.00%	68.00%
Unknown	0.00%	100.00%

Table 1.3.5 Have you ever taught any of the following? Hybrid law course during the Pandemic. Broken out by gender of respondent

Gender of respondent	Yes	No
Male	30.00%	70.00%
Female	38.00%	62.00%
Other	50.00%	50.00%

Table 1.3.6 Have you ever taught any of the following? Hybrid law course during the Pandemic. Broken out by public or private law school

Public or private law school	Yes	No
Public	25.93%	74.07%
Private	45.28%	54.72%

Table 1.3.7 Have you ever taught any of the following? Hybrid law course during the Pandemic. Broken out by # of courses taught last semester

# of courses taught last semester	Yes	No
None	18.52%	81.48%
One	30.00%	70.00%
Two	40.68%	59.32%
More than two	50.00%	50.00%

Table 1.3.8 Have you ever taught any of the following? Hybrid law course during the Pandemic. Broken out by ranking

Ranking	Yes	No
Top 20 law school	11.11%	88.89%
Somewhere in the 21-75 rank	30.91%	69.09%
76 to 250	47.83%	52.17%
Other	50.00%	50.00%

Table 1.3.9 Have you ever taught any of the following? Hybrid law course during the Pandemic. Broken out by political views

Political views	Yes	No
Conservative	42.86%	57.14%
Centrist	23.53%	76.47%
Liberal	38.46%	61.54%
Left of Liberal	30.00%	70.00%
Unknown	0.00%	100.00%

Table 1.4.1 Have you ever taught any of the following? Hybrid law course during the Pandemic.

	No Answer	Yes	No
Entire sample	0.00%	11.94%	88.06%

Table 1.4.2 Have you ever taught any of the following? Hybrid law course during the Pandemic. Broken out by law school enrollment

Law school enrollment	Yes	No
Less than 400	12.50%	87.50%
400+ - 550	3.13%	96.88%
550+ - 800	2.94%	97.06%
More than 800	27.78%	72.22%

Table 1.4.3 Have you ever taught any of the following? Hybrid law course during the Pandemic. Broken out by academic title

Academic title	Yes	No
Professor	18.03%	81.97%
Assistant/Associate Professor	14.29%	85.71%
Adjunct/Clinical Faculty	3.57%	96.43%
Emeritus	6.67%	93.33%
Other	0.00%	100.00%

Table 1.4.4 Have you ever taught any of the following? Hybrid law course during the Pandemic. Broken out by age of respondent

Age of respondent	Yes	No
Under 40	33.33%	66.67%
40-49	15.79%	84.21%
50-59	6.06%	93.94%
60 or over	12.00%	88.00%
Unknown	0.00%	100.00%

Table 1.4.5 Have you ever taught any of the following? Hybrid law course during the Pandemic. Broken out by gender of respondent

Gender of respondent	Yes	No
Male	8.75%	91.25%
Female	16.00%	84.00%
Other	25.00%	75.00%

Table 1.4.6 Have you ever taught any of the following? Hybrid law course during the Pandemic. Broken out by public or private law school

Public or private law school	Yes	No
Public	7.41%	92.59%
Private	18.87%	81.13%

Table 1.4.7 Have you ever taught any of the following? Hybrid law course during the Pandemic. Broken out by # of courses taught last semester

# of courses taught last semester	Yes	No
None	3.70%	96.30%
One	17.50%	82.50%
Two	11.86%	88.14%
More than two	12.50%	87.50%

Table 1.4.8 Have you ever taught any of the following? Hybrid law course during the Pandemic. Broken out by ranking

Ranking	Yes	No
Top 20 law school	3.70%	96.30%
Somewhere in the 21-75 rank	12.73%	87.27%
76 to 250	10.87%	89.13%
Other	50.00%	50.00%

Table 1.4.9 Have you ever taught any of the following? Hybrid law course during the Pandemic. Broken out by political views

Political views	Yes	No
Conservative	7.14%	92.86%
Centrist	8.82%	91.18%
Liberal	13.85%	86.15%
Left of Liberal	15.00%	85.00%
Unknown	0.00%	100.00%

Table 2.1 Have you taught an online or hybrid legal course within the past year?

	No Answer	Yes	No
Entire sample	8.96%	21.64%	69.40%

Table 2.2 Have you taught an online or hybrid legal course within the past year? Broken out by law school enrollment

Law school enrollment	No Answer	Yes	No
Less than 400	12.50%	18.75%	68.75%
400+ - 550	12.50%	15.63%	71.88%
550+ - 800	2.94%	17.65%	79.41%
More than 800	8.33%	33.33%	58.33%

Table 2.3 Have you taught an online or hybrid legal course within the past year? Broken out by academic title

Academic title	No Answer	Yes	No
Professor	8.20%	22.95%	68.85%
Assistant/Associate Professor	9.52%	23.81%	66.67%
Adjunct/Clinical Faculty	7.14%	21.43%	71.43%
Emeritus	13.33%	13.33%	73.33%
Other	11.11%	22.22%	66.67%

Table 2.4 Have you taught an online or hybrid legal course within the past year? Broken out by age of respondent

Age of respondent	No Answer	Yes	No
Under 40	16.67%	16.67%	66.67%
40-49	15.79%	15.79%	68.42%
50-59	0.00%	21.21%	78.79%
60 or over	10.67%	22.67%	66.67%
Unknown	0.00%	100.00%	0.00%

Table 2.5 Have you taught an online or hybrid legal course within the past year? Broken out by gender of respondent

Gender of respondent	No Answer	Yes	No
Male	11.25%	20.00%	68.75%
Female	6.00%	22.00%	72.00%
Other	0.00%	50.00%	50.00%

Table 2.6 Have you taught an online or hybrid legal course within the past year? Broken out by public or private law school

Public or private law school	No Answer	Yes	No
Public	11.11%	18.52%	70.37%
Private	5.66%	26.42%	67.92%

Table 2.7 Have you taught an online or hybrid legal course within the past year? Broken out by # of courses taught last semester

# of courses taught last semester	No Answer	Yes	No
None	7.41%	7.41%	85.19%
One	2.50%	27.50%	70.00%
Two	10.17%	25.42%	64.41%
More than two	37.50%	12.50%	50.00%

Table 2.8 Have you taught an online or hybrid legal course within the past year? Broken out by ranking

Ranking	No Answer	Yes	No
Top 20 law school	14.81%	14.81%	70.37%
Somewhere in the 21-75 rank	5.45%	16.36%	78.18%
76 to 250	6.52%	28.26%	65.22%
Other	33.33%	50.00%	16.67%

Table 2.9 Have you taught an online or hybrid legal course within the past year? Broken out by political views

Political views	No Answer	Yes	No
Conservative	7.14%	21.43%	71.43%
Centrist	14.71%	32.35%	52.94%
Liberal	7.69%	21.54%	70.77%
Left of Liberal	5.00%	5.00%	90.00%
Unknown	0.00%	0.00%	100.00%

Table 3.1 In general what do you think of the general quality of online legal education relative to traditional courses at your institution?

	No Answer	Much better	Better	About the same	Worse	Much worse
Entire sample	11.19%	4.48%	5.22%	23.13%	38.81%	17.16%

Table 3.2 In general what do you think of the general quality of online legal education relative to traditional courses at your institution? Broken out by law school enrollment

Law school enrollment	No Answer	Much better	Better	About the same	Worse	Much worse
Less than 400	15.63%	0.00%	3.13%	28.13%	34.38%	18.75%
400+ - 550	12.50%	6.25%	6.25%	18.75%	46.88%	9.38%
550+ - 800	5.88%	5.88%	2.94%	29.41%	35.29%	20.59%
More than 800	11.11%	5.56%	8.33%	16.67%	38.89%	19.44%

Table 3.3 In general what do you think of the general quality of online legal education relative to traditional courses at your institution? Broken out by academic title

Academic title	No Answer	Much better	Better	About the same	Worse	Much worse
Professor	8.20%	3.28%	3.28%	26.23%	39.34%	19.67%
Assistant/Associate Professor	9.52%	4.76%	9.52%	9.52%	57.14%	9.52%
Adjunct/Clinical Faculty	14.29%	7.14%	3.57%	25.00%	32.14%	17.86%
Emeritus	20.00%	0.00%	13.33%	26.67%	26.67%	13.33%
Other	11.11%	11.11%	0.00%	22.22%	33.33%	22.22%

Table 3.4 In general what do you think of the general quality of online legal education relative to traditional courses at your institution? Broken out by age of respondent

Age of respondent	No Answer	Much better	Better	About the same	Worse	Much worse
Under 40	33.33%	0.00%	16.67%	0.00%	50.00%	0.00%
40-49	15.79%	5.26%	15.79%	15.79%	42.11%	5.26%
50-59	6.06%	6.06%	3.03%	18.18%	51.52%	15.15%
60 or over	10.67%	4.00%	2.67%	28.00%	32.00%	22.67%
Unknown	0.00%	0.00%	0.00%	100.00%	0.00%	0.00%

Table 3.5 In general what do you think of the general quality of online legal education relative to traditional courses at your institution? Broken out by gender of respondent

Gender of respondent	No Answer	Much better	Better	About the same	Worse	Much worse
Male	12.50%	2.50%	2.50%	20.00%	42.50%	20.00%
Female	10.00%	8.00%	10.00%	24.00%	36.00%	12.00%
Other	0.00%	0.00%	0.00%	75.00%	0.00%	25.00%

Table 3.6 In general what do you think of the general quality of online legal education relative to traditional courses at your institution? Broken out by public or private law school

Public or private law school	No Answer	Much better	Better	About the same	Worse	Much worse
Public	13.58%	4.94%	3.70%	18.52%	41.98%	17.28%
Private	7.55%	3.77%	7.55%	30.19%	33.96%	16.98%

Table 3.7 In general what do you think of the general quality of online legal education relative to traditional courses at your institution? Broken out by # of courses taught last semester

# of courses taught last semester	No Answer	Much better	Better	About the same	Worse	Much worse
None	11.11%	7.41%	7.41%	22.22%	25.93%	25.93%
One	5.00%	7.50%	10.00%	17.50%	42.50%	17.50%
Two	10.17%	1.69%	1.69%	27.12%	45.76%	13.56%
More than two	50.00%	0.00%	0.00%	25.00%	12.50%	12.50%

Table 3.8 In general what do you think of the general quality of online legal education relative to traditional courses at your institution? Broken out by ranking

Ranking	No Answer	Much better	Better	About the same	Worse	Much worse
Top 20 law school	25.93%	3.70%	0.00%	25.93%	18.52%	25.93%
Somewhere in the 21-75 rank	3.64%	7.27%	7.27%	20.00%	47.27%	14.55%
76 to 250	6.52%	2.17%	4.35%	26.09%	43.48%	17.39%
Other	50.00%	0.00%	16.67%	16.67%	16.67%	0.00%

Table 3.9 In general what do you think of the general quality of online legal education relative to traditional courses at your institution? Broken out by political views

Political views	No Answer	Much better	Better	About the same	Worse	Much worse
Conservative	14.29%	0.00%	0.00%	7.14%	64.29%	14.29%
Centrist	14.71%	8.82%	5.88%	23.53%	35.29%	11.76%
Liberal	10.77%	3.08%	6.15%	27.69%	35.38%	16.92%
Left of Liberal	5.00%	5.00%	5.00%	15.00%	40.00%	30.00%
Unknown	0.00%	0.00%	0.00%	100.00%	0.00%	0.00%

Table 4.1 How extensively is your law school using online legal education?

	No Answer	A great deal	A lot	A moderate amount	A little	None at all
Entire sample	8.96%	2.24%	7.46%	23.88%	46.27%	11.19%

Table 4.2 How extensively is your law school using online legal education? Broken out by law school enrollment

Law school enrollment	No Answer	A great deal	A lot	A moderate amount	A little	None at all
Less than 400	12.50%	3.13%	6.25%	12.50%	53.13%	12.50%
400+ - 550	9.38%	0.00%	6.25%	28.13%	53.13%	3.13%
550+ - 800	5.88%	0.00%	5.88%	35.29%	44.12%	8.82%
More than 800	8.33%	5.56%	11.11%	19.44%	36.11%	19.44%

Table 4.3 How extensively is your law school using online legal education? Broken out by academic title

Academic title	No Answer	A great deal	A lot	A moderate amount	A little	None at all
Professor	8.20%	1.64%	9.84%	22.95%	47.54%	9.84%
Assistant/Associate Professor	9.52%	9.52%	4.76%	14.29%	52.38%	9.52%
Adjunct/Clinical Faculty	10.71%	0.00%	3.57%	28.57%	46.43%	10.71%
Emeritus	6.67%	0.00%	6.67%	33.33%	33.33%	20.00%
Other	11.11%	0.00%	11.11%	22.22%	44.44%	11.11%

Table 4.4 How extensively is your law school using online legal education? Broken out by age of respondent

Age of respondent	No Answer	A great deal	A lot	A moderate amount	A little	None at all
Under 40	33.33%	16.67%	0.00%	16.67%	33.33%	0.00%
40-49	15.79%	0.00%	0.00%	5.26%	68.42%	10.53%
50-59	0.00%	6.06%	9.09%	21.21%	51.52%	12.12%
60 or over	9.33%	0.00%	9.33%	30.67%	38.67%	12.00%
Unknown	0.00%	0.00%	0.00%	0.00%	100.00%	0.00%

Table 4.5 How extensively is your law school using online legal education? Broken out by gender of respondent

Gender of respondent	No Answer	A great deal	A lot	A moderate amount	A little	None at all
Male	10.00%	1.25%	7.50%	25.00%	42.50%	13.75%
Female	8.00%	4.00%	6.00%	22.00%	52.00%	8.00%
Other	0.00%	0.00%	25.00%	25.00%	50.00%	0.00%

Table 4.6 How extensively is your law school using online legal education? Broken out by public or private law school

Public or private law school	No Answer	A great deal	A lot	A moderate amount	A little	None at all
Public	11.11%	0.00%	7.41%	23.46%	48.15%	9.88%
Private	5.66%	5.66%	7.55%	24.53%	43.40%	13.21%

Table 4.7 How extensively is your law school using online legal education? Broken out by # of courses taught last semester

# of courses taught last semester	No Answer	A great deal	A lot	A moderate amount	A little	None at all
None	3.70%	0.00%	11.11%	25.93%	37.04%	22.22%
One	5.00%	2.50%	7.50%	30.00%	47.50%	7.50%
Two	10.17%	3.39%	5.08%	20.34%	50.85%	10.17%
More than two	37.50%	0.00%	12.50%	12.50%	37.50%	0.00%

Table 4.8 How extensively is your law school using online legal education? Broken out by ranking

Ranking	No Answer	A great deal	A lot	A moderate amount	A little	None at all
Top 20 law school	18.52%	0.00%	3.70%	14.81%	40.74%	22.22%
Somewhere in the 21-75 rank	3.64%	0.00%	7.27%	29.09%	49.09%	10.91%
76 to 250	6.52%	4.35%	6.52%	26.09%	50.00%	6.52%
Other	33.33%	16.67%	33.33%	0.00%	16.67%	0.00%

Table 4.9 How extensively is your law school using online legal education? Broken out by political views

Political views	No Answer	A great deal	A lot	A moderate amount	A little	None at all
Conservative	7.14%	0.00%	14.29%	28.57%	42.86%	7.14%
Centrist	14.71%	2.94%	8.82%	23.53%	44.12%	5.88%
Liberal	7.69%	3.08%	7.69%	26.15%	44.62%	10.77%
Left of Liberal	5.00%	0.00%	0.00%	15.00%	55.00%	25.00%
Unknown	0.00%	0.00%	0.00%	0.00%	100.00%	0.00%

Table 5.1 Do you agree: My law school should significantly increase its use of online legal education.

	No Answer	Strongly agree	Agree	Neither agree nor disagree	Disagree	Strongly disagree
Entire sample	8.96%	8.21%	13.43%	16.42%	24.63%	28.36%

Table 5.2 Do you agree: My law school should significantly increase its use of online legal education. Broken out by law school enrollment

Law school enrollment	No Answer	Strongly agree	Agree	Neither agree nor disagree	Disagree	Strongly disagree
Less than 400	12.50%	6.25%	12.50%	21.88%	18.75%	28.13%
400+ - 550	9.38%	9.38%	12.50%	21.88%	21.88%	25.00%
550+ - 800	5.88%	2.94%	20.59%	14.71%	29.41%	26.47%
More than 800	8.33%	13.89%	8.33%	8.33%	27.78%	33.33%

Table 5.3 Do you agree: My law school should significantly increase its use of online legal education. Broken out by academic title

Academic title	No Answer	Strongly agree	Agree	Neither agree nor disagree	Disagree	Strongly disagree
Professor	8.20%	9.84%	18.03%	9.84%	26.23%	27.87%
Assistant/ Associate Professor	9.52%	14.29%	9.52%	19.05%	19.05%	28.57%
Adjunct/ Clinical Faculty	10.71%	3.57%	14.29%	21.43%	32.14%	17.86%
Emeritus	6.67%	0.00%	6.67%	20.00%	26.67%	40.00%
Other	11.11%	11.11%	0.00%	33.33%	0.00%	44.44%

Table 5.4 Do you agree: My law school should significantly increase its use of online legal education. Broken out by age of respondent

Age of respondent	No Answer	Strongly agree	Agree	Neither agree nor disagree	Disagree	Strongly disagree
Under 40	33.33%	0.00%	0.00%	16.67%	16.67%	33.33%
40-49	15.79%	21.05%	5.26%	10.53%	36.84%	10.53%
50-59	0.00%	6.06%	21.21%	18.18%	24.24%	30.30%
60 or over	9.33%	5.33%	13.33%	17.33%	22.67%	32.00%
Unknown	0.00%	100.00%	0.00%	0.00%	0.00%	0.00%

Table 5.5 Do you agree: My law school should significantly increase its use of online legal education. Broken out by gender of respondent

Gender of respondent	No Answer	Strongly agree	Agree	Neither agree nor disagree	Disagree	Strongly disagree
Male	10.00%	5.00%	12.50%	15.00%	25.00%	32.50%
Female	8.00%	10.00%	14.00%	20.00%	24.00%	24.00%
Other	0.00%	50.00%	25.00%	0.00%	25.00%	0.00%

Table 5.6 Do you agree: My law school should significantly increase its use of online legal education. Broken out by public or private law school

Public or private law school	No Answer	Strongly agree	Agree	Neither agree nor disagree	Disagree	Strongly disagree
Public	11.11%	6.17%	8.64%	18.52%	24.69%	30.86%
Private	5.66%	11.32%	20.75%	13.21%	24.53%	24.53%

Table 5.7 Do you agree: My law school should significantly increase its use of online legal education. Broken out by # of courses taught last semester

# of courses taught last semester	No Answer	Strongly agree	Agree	Neither agree nor disagree	Disagree	Strongly disagree
None	3.70%	7.41%	7.41%	25.93%	18.52%	37.04%
One	5.00%	7.50%	15.00%	20.00%	22.50%	30.00%
Two	10.17%	8.47%	15.25%	11.86%	27.12%	27.12%
More than two	37.50%	12.50%	12.50%	0.00%	37.50%	0.00%

Table 5.8 Do you agree: My law school should significantly increase its use of online legal education. Broken out by ranking

Ranking	No Answer	Strongly agree	Agree	Neither agree nor disagree	Disagree	Strongly disagree
Top 20 law school	18.52%	0.00%	18.52%	11.11%	25.93%	25.93%
Somewhere in the 21-75 rank	3.64%	10.91%	10.91%	18.18%	25.45%	30.91%
76 to 250	6.52%	8.70%	15.22%	17.39%	23.91%	28.26%
Other	33.33%	16.67%	0.00%	16.67%	16.67%	16.67%

Table 5.9 Do you agree: My law school should significantly increase its use of online legal education. Broken out by political views

Political views	No Answer	Strongly agree	Agree	Neither agree nor disagree	Disagree	Strongly disagree
Conservative	7.14%	0.00%	7.14%	7.14%	50.00%	28.57%
Centrist	14.71%	17.65%	14.71%	17.65%	14.71%	20.59%
Liberal	7.69%	4.62%	16.92%	15.38%	26.15%	29.23%
Left of Liberal	5.00%	10.00%	5.00%	25.00%	15.00%	40.00%
Unknown	0.00%	0.00%	0.00%	0.00%	100.00%	0.00%

How and for what should online legal education be used at your institution?

Top 20 law school

1 Online, virtual, or "Zoom" classes are a joke. Just amazed that tuition-paying students put up with them and that we haven't been sued yet for pro-rata tuition adjustments.
2 Online platforms are great for skills-based legal courses.
3 When in person instruction is not feasible.
4 responding to weather related emergencies and rare needs to be remote.
5 Rarely and only for extenuating circumstances.
6 Raising awareness in general population (both in the US and internationally) of law, in practical terms. immigration law, refugee law, torts, contracts, criminal law
7 It should not be used,
8 Only when absolutely necessary
9 It worked surprisingly well with a class of modest size and highly motivated students. But everyone preferred to get back in person. Online should be reserved for special situations, such as a joint-enrollment course with students from two or more law schools. Or a pandemic.
10 Emergencies

Somewhere in the 21-75 rank

1 To bring the most qualified instructors on board who live or work too far from the law school to teach on person
2 Only as a last resort to cover an important course that cannot be taught in house.
3 Online education is a profit maker. Using it for ancillary programs (such the MSL) probably cannot be avoided (if only for cynical reasons). But people need to learn in person, in interaction with others (both teachers and fellow students), and in the context of a personal relationship with an experienced lawyer/teacher. There is no meaningful substitute.
4 Pandemics, global thermonuclear war....
5 We devote significant faculty and other resources to running a part-time evening program in which 20 students matriculate in a good year, out of whom 5-10 students will switch to the full-time program after their 1L year. I think we could reduce the burden of staffing the evening part-time program with full-time faculty by switching to an online part-time program, elective classes of which would be open to full-time students as well.
6 AI tutoring and instruction should be used. Zoom classes are ineffective.
7 I know that online legal education makes it more accessible to people that may not otherwise be able to avail themselves of a legal education. However, having online, hybrid, and in-person, I do feel that in-

person courses are superior. However, it is unlikely that education can remain only in-person in the future.

8 I believe we should integrate more fully into our curriculum. Many of our students work or commute, and these courses offer them more flexibility without diminishing their learning experience.

9 Supplemental instruction

10 We use it for some graduate programs and makeup days

11 Certificate programs for attorneys, masters in law program for those without JDs. paralegal programs

12 Seminars

13 For bringing in remote students and remote speakers, collaborating with other students/professors across great distances

14 When the law school building is closed due to weather or other emergencies.

15 Online education is inferior. It should be used sparingly.

16 As an accommodation for faculty and students who need to be remote

17 Only when necessary

18 It should be a regular and frequent part of the education.

19 To supplement class time. Our courses are too hurried.

20 Pandemics

21 Summer classes

22 As a supplement to in-person courses

23 Summer class offerings

24 Quality asynchronous course are good. Most I have seen are low quality. Hybrid courses do not work well because online students are easily overlooked.

25 Courses that bring in guests like seminars and symposia. Whenever faculty thinks a class should be online

26 To expand the availability of legal education to otherwise underserved communities

27 Continuing education

28 Evening students; unfortunately there are regulatory constraints, especially for LL.M. students.

29 Some graduate level courses for LL.M. students who already have JDs.

30 It should not - it is terrible and everyone involved knows It but it is so much less work that faculty are on board despite the harm to the students

76 to 250

1 Only for illness, weather, or necessary conflicts
2 It really depends on so many factors. You have to think about your learning objectives, teaching styles, and nature of the topics vis a vis available tools on the front end, when developing the course, rather than just retrofit a course, for online tools to make for powerful learning. Although, as a general rule, I think Manny course could benefit from the
3 Firmly believe in person law school education is superior and necessary
4 For courses for which we don't have instructors.
5 Only for emergencies when in-person not possible.
6 Online legal education is extremely helpful (1) for part-time students, (2) for allowing the school to bring in adjuncts that may not be locally based, and (3) provide more class options when space would not allow each option to be held on-campus at the same time.
7 Upper-level required courses and electives.
8 To avail students of opportunities to spend a semester off site while continuing to take courses.
9 To broaden content availability, to minimize conflicts
10 Raising revenue through CLE; maybe some carefully curated upper-level courses, for which online makes sense; cautious expansion of hybrid classes to facilitate access to legal education and to work alongside programs such as non-local field placement.
11 For limited summer course offerings. I think it would be valuable for writing and research classes.
12 Instructors should have more latitude to use it when they believe it furthers pedagogical purposes.
13 This survey is taking many times longer than the email estimate I relied on when I started the survey. I don't have time to type any additional answers.
14 Summer courses while students are working
15 Online was great for the pandemic; in other situations, it is less good
16 Accommodate disability
17 It should be embraced for skills and heavily practice-centered and hybrid for basics bar courses.
18 For graduate and continuing education
19 As a way to accommodate students who are actually unable to attend in person.
20 Small classes, part time students
21 With adequate training, online education could be used to open pathways for marginalized students who do not otherwise have easy access to legal education due to work and family commitments. Any class, with adequate preparation, can be taught online. The online platform is so dynamic that it is actually more effective for me to teach online than in person.
22 CLE
23 It should be limited to certain types of upper level courses and electives.

24 We have a leading model for online and hybrid legal education. We prioritize pedagogy and have an exceptional student body. We should keep doing what we are doing.

25 Only for courses that can reliably be enrolled with highly motivated, independent students.

www.ingramcontent.com/pod-product-compliance
Lightning Source LLC
LaVergne TN
LVHW080528210926
848481LV00022B/3644